# THE
# CAK
# PUDDINGS
## COOKBOOK

# THE POCKET
# CAKES AND
# PUDDINGS
# COOKBOOK

Syd Pemberton

PENGUIN BOOKS

*Front-cover photograph: Pineapple Blitztorte (page 48); back-cover photograph: Rich Food Processor Chocolate Cake (page 54)*

Penguin Books Australia Ltd
487 Maroondah Highway, PO Box 257
Ringwood, Victoria 3134, Australia
Penguin Books Ltd
Harmondsworth, Middlesex, England
Penguin Putnam Inc.
375 Hudson Street, New York, New York 10014, USA
Penguin Books Canada Limited
10 Alcorn Avenue, Toronto, Ontario, Canada M4V 3B2
Penguin Books (NZ) Ltd
Cnr Rosedale and Airborne Roads, Albany, Auckland, New Zealand
Penguin Books (South Africa) (Pty) Ltd
5 Watkins Street, Denver Ext 4, 2094, South Africa
Penguin Books India (P) Ltd
11, Community Centre, Panchsheel Park, New Delhi 110 017, India

First published by Penguin Books Australia 2000

10 9 8 7 6 5 4 3 2 1

Copyright © Penguin Books Australia Ltd, 2000

Designed by Marina Messiha, Penguin Design Studio
Cover photography by Simon Griffiths
Food styling and preparation by Virginia Dowzer
Illustrated by Michelle Ryan
Typeset in 8.5/12pt Giovanni by Midland Typesetters Pty Ltd, Maryborough, Victoria
Printed in Australia by Australian Print Group, Maryborough, Victoria

National Library of Australia
Cataloguing-in-Publication data:

Pemberton, Syd.
  The pocket cakes and puddings cookbook.
  Includes index.
  ISBN 0 14 028244 0.
  1. Puddings. 2. Cakes. I. Title.

642.8653

www.penguin.com.au

# CONTENTS

# INTRODUCTION

Cake baking is a wonderfully rewarding cooking skill that many of us have picked up from an early age. We all remember helping Mum in the kitchen, stirring the cake batter and being lucky enough to lick the spoon or the bowl at the end of mixing – yummy!

There is nothing more delightful than coming home to a kitchen that smells of a freshly baked cake, not long out of the oven, and cutting into it while it's still warm. Delicious cakes pop up at afternoon teas, fund-raising stalls, dinner parties, special celebrations, as a birthday gift or just as a 'thank you'! They don't have to be fancy – a simple dusting of icing sugar on top is often all they need to make them special.

Warm puddings are the sort of dessert that we also learnt how to cook at an early age with Mum or Granny in the kitchen. A simple apple crumble or baked custard is both easy to make and can be a very satisfying finish to any meal. The delight of starting off with a 'family' recipe and then experimenting with some different ingredients will ensure the old-fashioned recipes continue to be re-invented. Who hasn't had a conversation with friends about how your mum made her baked apples?

Puddings are nostalgic and remind us of our childhood. They have a place in the history of eating and no one ever seems to get tired of them.

All the recipes in this book were designed to be quick

and easy to prepare. The cake recipes follow simple methods that don't require fancy tins or equipment. And the pudding recipes are drawn from many of my family favourites, which have passed the test of time. Some, of course, have been adapted to include more modern ingredients, which I am sure you will enjoy. All my taste-testers gave the 'thumbs up' and I have had enormous fun baking cakes and puddings for such an appreciative audience!

## ✽ Some Cake-making Tips

- Prepare the tin before making the cake batter by lining it with a non-stick baking paper (just the base is fine for tins with a non-stick finish), or lightly greasing, or lightly greasing and then dusting with flour – according to the recipe.
- Use the correct size of tin, as specified in the recipe (as a guide the batter should fill the tin to about half the depth, to ensure that it does not rise over the sides).
- Preheat the oven to the recommended cooking temperature.
- Measure all the ingredients out first, before starting to make the cake batter.
- Eggs, butter, margarine, and oil are best used at room temperature.
- The egg size used in most recipes is medium

(approximately 60g); where large size is specified, use 65g eggs.

- Test the cake near the end of the recommended baking time, to see if it's cooked through. Use a wooden skewer to pierce the middle of the cake – if the skewer comes out clean the cake is ready. Alternatively, press the cake gently with your fingers – if the cake springs back, it's cooked. Opening the door of the oven in the last 5 minutes of cooking time should not cause the cake to sink.
- Always remove cakes from the oven after baking and allow to cool.

## The Language of Cake- and Pudding-making

*To beat* – vigorous mixing with a spoon or electric mixer

*To blend* – combine one ingredient with another until completely mixed together, either using a fork, wooden spoon or electric mixer

*To cream* – usually refers to butter or fat, alone or mixed with sugar until light, pale yellow and fluffy (takes 3–4 minutes)

*To fold in* – carefully incorporate one mixture into another – usually a light one such as whipped egg whites into a heavier mixture; folding involves gently 'drawing' a figure of eight with a metal spoon and being careful not to knock the air out of the lighter mixture

*To stir* – mix carefully in a circular motion to combine

*To whip* – beat rapidly with a whisk or electric mixer to incorporate as much air as possible; cream or egg whites are examples of ingredients that are whipped

*To cook in a 'bain marie'* (water bath) – the pudding dish is placed in a baking tin filled with hot water reaching halfway up the sides of the dish; this method protects any delicate mixture that requires a gentle, indirect heat

*To bake blind* – pastry is precooked by lining it with non-stick baking paper, weighing it down with uncooked rice or dried pulses and baking it in the oven

## ✥ Cake-making Equipment

The basic equipment for cooking cakes includes:

- round springform cake tins, square cake tins and loaf tins
- metric measuring spoons
- metric measuring cups
- metric kitchen scales
- two or three mixing bowls
- electric whisk or beater
- food processor
- medium saucepan
- wooden spoons
- spatulas
- non-stick baking paper
- sieve
- wire cake rack

## ☙ Cake Tin Sizes

A 20-cm round cake tin produces 6–8 portions.

A 23-cm round cake tin produces 8–12 portions.

A 23-cm square cake tin produces 10–12 portions.

A 30-cm × 20-cm lamington pan produces 6–8 portions.

A 25-cm × 15-cm loaf pan produces 10–12 portions.

# A FEW BASIC RECIPES

## ✍ Butterscotch Sauce

¾ cup castor sugar
¼ cup boiling water
¾ cup brown sugar
50 g butter
pure vanilla extract
100 ml cream

Dissolve the castor sugar in a saucepan over a gentle heat and bring to the boil. Cook until the syrup turns a golden brown.

Off the heat, pour in the boiling water and stir. Stir in the brown sugar and butter and return to the heat until the mixture is smooth and the sugar is dissolved. Stir in the vanilla and cream and cool until ready to serve.

## ✍ Caramel Rum Sauce

½ cup sugar
2 tablespoons water
1 tablespoon dark rum
2 tablespoons butter
½ cup cream

In a heavy-bottomed saucepan, slowly heat the sugar and water, stirring until the sugar is melted. Increase the heat and cook until the syrup starts to caramelise, turning a light golden colour. Remove from the heat and stir in the dark rum, butter and cream. Whisk over a low heat until the sauce is smooth. Cool. The sauce can be made in advance and refrigerated until ready to use.

## ❧ Coffee Icing

325 g icing sugar
200 g softened butter
2 teaspoons instant coffee dissolved in 2 tablespoons
    boiling water

Place the icing sugar in a food processor and pulse to remove any lumps. Add the butter and coffee. Process until smooth.

## ❧ Cream Cheese Icing

250 g softened cream cheese
50 g softened butter
1 teaspoon vanilla
500 g icing sugar

Using a food processor or electric mixer, blend the cream cheese and softened butter. Add the vanilla, then mix in the icing sugar until smooth. Refrigerate until ready to use.

Use a spatula to spread the icing over the top and sides of the cake.

## 🌱 Hot Chocolate Sauce

100 g dark chocolate, broken into small pieces
150 ml cream

Place the chocolate and cream in a saucepan over a gentle heat. Cook, stirring constantly, until the chocolate has melted and the sauce is smooth and glossy.

## 🌱 Lemon Curd

Makes about 1 cup
grated zest and juice of 2 lemons
75 g castor sugar
1 tablespoon cornflour
4 egg yolks

Combine the lemon juice, sugar and cornflour in a saucepan. Slowly bring to the boil and stir until mixture thickens. Remove from the heat and whisk in the egg yolks

and lemon zest. Return to a gentle heat and cook for
2–3 minutes. Remove and allow to cool.

## ✼ Melba Sauce

300 g tinned or frozen raspberries (defrosted)
2 tablespoons redcurrant jelly
1/2 tablespoon icing sugar
1 tablespoon arrowroot, mixed with 1 tablespoon cold
    water

Rub the raspberries through a sieve to remove all the seeds.
Place in a saucepan and add the redcurrant jelly and icing
sugar. Slowly bring to the boil; then turn the heat down
and stir in the arrowroot. Continue stirring until the sauce
has thickened (2–3 minutes).

## ✼ Orange Icing

225 g softened, unsalted butter
225 g icing sugar
grated zest and juice of 1/2 an orange

In a food processor or electric mixer, cream the butter and
icing sugar until light and fluffy. Slowly mix in the orange
zest and juice until smooth.

## ❦ Passionfruit Sauce

150 ml passionfruit pulp
50 g castor sugar
zest and juice of 1 orange

Heat all the ingredients in a small saucepan, stirring until
the sugar has melted. Bring to the boil and cook for
1 minute. Remove and strain into a bowl. Allow to cool.

## ❦ Pouring Custard

2 eggs
1 tablespoon castor sugar
250 ml milk
a few drops of vanilla extract

Using a whisk, mix the eggs and sugar lightly. Heat the
milk and vanilla extract in a saucepan until just warmed
through; then remove from the heat and pour over the
eggs.

Tip the custard sauce back into the saucepan and, stirring
all the time, slowly bring to the boil. Turn down
immediately to a simmer and cook, still stirring constantly,
until the custard is thick enough to coat the back of a
spoon.

Serve hot or cold.

# ✎ Rhubarb Sauce

4 stalks rhubarb, trimmed and cut into small pieces
¼ cup brown sugar
2 tablespoons orange juice

Cook the rhubarb with the sugar and orange juice in a
saucepan over a gentle heat for 8–10 minutes or until soft.
Remove and cool to room temperature.

# CAKES

# ✌ Almond Sponge

*6 eggs, separated*
*¹/₃ cup castor sugar*
*3 tablespoons orange juice*
*¹/₄ teaspoon vanilla extract*
*²/₃ cup plain flour*
*1¹/₂ cups finely ground almonds*
*1 tablespoon finely grated orange zest*
*pinch of salt*
*1 teaspoon cream of tartar*
*¹/₃ cup castor sugar*
*fresh berries*

Preheat the oven to 150°C. Lightly butter and flour a 25-cm
bundt pan.

Using an electric mixer, whisk the egg yolks and castor
sugar until thick and creamy. Add the orange juice and
vanilla extract. Combine the sifted flour, almonds, orange
rind and pinch of salt. Fold into the egg-yolk mixture.
Whisk the egg whites and cream of tartar until soft peaks
form. Slowly whisk in the sugar until glossy. Fold into the
cake batter until combined. Pour the batter into the
prepared pan. Bake for 45–50 minutes.

Cool in the pan, then invert onto a serving platter and
spoon the berries into the middle.

Serve with pouring cream.

# ✅ Apple and Cinnamon Cake

*1 cup self-raising flour*
*2 tablespoons castor sugar*
*60 g butter, softened*
*1 egg, lightly beaten*
*⅓ cup milk*

Topping
*200 g green apples, peeled, cored and thinly sliced*
*½ teaspoon ground cinnamon*
*1 teaspoon cornflour*
*30 g melted butter*

Preheat the oven to 180°C. Lightly grease a 23-cm round springform cake tin and line the base with non-stick baking paper.

Sift the flour and sugar into a mixing bowl. Add the butter and cut into the flour until mixture resembles coarse breadcrumbs. Stir in the egg and milk and beat to a smooth batter. Spread over the base of the prepared tin.

Combine the apples, cinnamon and cornflour in a bowl. Arrange on top of the cake batter. Drizzle melted butter over the top.

Bake for 45 minutes or until cooked through. Cool in the tin on a rack. Remove from the tin when cold.

# ❧ Apple, Rum and Date Cake

$^1/_2$ cup chopped dates, soaked in $^1/_4$ cup rum
140 g butter
$1^1/_2$ cups castor sugar
3 eggs
2 cups self-raising flour
$^1/_2$ teaspoon ground nutmeg
$^1/_2$ teaspoon ground cinnamon
$^1/_2$ teaspoon ground ginger
$^1/_2$ teaspoon ground cloves
pinch of salt
1 teaspoon baking powder
2 cups chopped apples
2 cups chopped walnuts

Preheat the oven to 180°C. Lightly grease a 23-cm springform cake tin and line the base with non-stick baking paper.

Place the dates and rum in a small saucepan. Cook for 5 minutes over a gentle heat. Remove; then cool.

Cream the butter and sugar in a mixing bowl until light and fluffy. Add the eggs one at a time until well combined.

Sift all the dry ingredients into a mixing bowl. Coat the walnuts and apples with a little flour. Fold the dry ingredients, then the apples and walnuts into the butter mixture. Stir through the dates.

Pour into the prepared tin and bake for 1 hour or until cooked through. Cool in the tin; then turn out onto a rack.

Serve with whipped cream.

# ✑ Banana and Buttermilk Cake

*200 g unsalted butter*
*1 cup castor sugar*
*3 large eggs*
*3 ripe bananas, well mashed*
*2 teaspoons vanilla extract*
*1 cup buttermilk*
*1¾ cups self-raising flour*
*1 teaspoon bicarbonate of soda*
*pinch of salt*

Preheat the oven to 180°C. Lightly grease a 23-cm springform cake tin and line the base with non-stick baking paper.

Cream the butter and sugar until light and fluffy. Add the eggs, mashed bananas, vanilla extract and buttermilk. Sift the flour, bicarbonate of soda and salt into another bowl. Stir the flour mixture into the batter and mix until smooth.

Pour into the prepared tin and bake for 45 minutes or until cooked through.

Cool in the tin for 10 minutes. Turn out onto a rack and cool for 10 minutes more.

Serve warm with Butterscotch Sauce (see page 6).

# ✐ Blueberry and Ricotta Cake

*60 g butter, melted*
*½ cup castor sugar*
*1 egg*
*⅔ cup sour cream*
*½ teaspoon vanilla extract*
*1 cup self-raising flour*

Topping
*1 cup icing sugar*
*225 g ricotta cheese*
*1 egg*
*2 tablespoons fresh lemon juice*
*2 cups fresh blueberries*

Preheat the oven to 180°C. Lightly butter and flour a 22-cm springform cake tin.

Using an electric mixer, beat the butter, sugar and egg together for about 1 minute until pale and thick. Mix in the sour cream, vanilla extract and sifted flour.

Spoon the batter into the prepared tin and bake for 20 minutes or until lightly browned and risen.

Meanwhile, beat the icing sugar, ricotta, egg and lemon juice together until smooth. Pour onto the hot cake and sprinkle the blueberries over the top. Return to the oven and bake for a further 30 minutes or until the cake topping is set and lightly browned. Cool in the tin on a rack.

Serve warm or at room temperature.

## Carol's Very Moist Carrot Cake

*2 cups plain flour*
*2 teaspoons bicarbonate of soda*
*2 teaspoons baking powder*
*2 teaspoons ground cinnamon*
*1 teaspoon salt*
*2 cups castor sugar*
*1 cup chopped walnuts*
*1½ cups light vegetable oil*
*4 eggs*
*3 cups grated, peeled carrots*
*walnut halves, for decoration*

Preheat the oven to 175°C. Line a 23-cm square cake tin with non-stick baking paper.

Sift the flour into a large mixing bowl with the bicarbonate of soda, baking powder, cinnamon and salt. Stir in the sugar and walnuts. In another bowl, mix the oil and eggs until well combined. Stir in the carrots.

Pour the wet mixture into the dry ingredients and mix to form a smooth batter. Pour into the prepared tin and bake for 1 hour or until cooked through. Cool for 5 minutes before turning out onto a rack.

When completely cold, ice the top and sides of the cake with Cream Cheese Icing (see page 7) and decorate with a few walnut halves.

# ❧ Chocolate Chip Cake

*200 g softened butter*
*200 g castor sugar*
*3 eggs, lightly beaten*
*275 g self-raising flour, sifted*
*150 g dark chocolate dots, or roughly chopped*
    *dark cooking chocolate*
*50 g ground almonds*
*2 tablespoons milk*
*25 g chopped almonds*

Preheat the oven to 180°C. Lightly grease a 20-cm round springform cake tin and line the base with non-stick baking paper.

Cream the butter and sugar until light and fluffy. Add the eggs a little at a time, alternating with a tablespoon of flour. Beat well to make a light batter; then fold in the rest of the flour, chocolate, ground almonds and milk. Sprinkle the chopped almonds over the top.

Pour the mixture into the prepared tin and bake for 1½ hours or until cooked through. Cool in the tin for 5 minutes before turning out onto a rack.

# ✈ Chocolate, Hazelnut and Ricotta Cheesecake

Base
*50 g finely chopped hazelnuts*
*100 g sweet biscuit crumbs*
*75 g melted butter*

Topping
*2 eggs, separated*
*35 g castor sugar*
*175 g ricotta cheese*
*20 g ground hazelnuts*
*75 ml cream*
*15 g cocoa powder*
*1 teaspoon dark rum*
*icing sugar, for dusting*

Preheat the oven to 170°C. Lightly grease a 20-cm spring-form cake tin and line the base with non-stick baking paper.

Combine the base ingredients and press into the base of the prepared tin.

Whisk the egg yolks and sugar until thick and creamy. Beat in the ricotta, ground hazelnuts, cream and cocoa powder. Stir in the dark rum.

Whip the egg whites until stiff and carefully fold through the chocolate mixture. Pour into the prepared tin and bake for 1 hour or until lightly risen and just firm to touch.

Cool a little before removing from the tin. Dust liberally with icing sugar before serving.

## 🥄 Chocolate Mousse Cake

*225 g dark cooking chocolate, broken into small pieces*
*125 g unsalted butter*
*7 eggs, separated*
*½ cup castor sugar*
*¼ cup brandy*
*pinch of salt*
*icing sugar, for dusting*

Preheat the oven to 160°C. Lightly grease a 23-cm springform cake tin and line the base with non-stick baking paper.

Place the chocolate and butter in a bowl, set over a saucepan of simmering water and stir until melted. Remove and cool a little.

Using an electric mixer, beat the egg yolks and sugar until pale and thick (3–4 minutes). Stir in the cooled chocolate mixture and brandy. In another bowl, whip the egg whites with a pinch of salt until stiff. Take two large spoonfuls of the egg-white mixture and carefully mix this through the chocolate mixture. Tip the chocolate mixture into the egg-white mixture and fold through. Spoon into the prepared tin and bake for 30–35 minutes or until cooked.

Cool in the tin on a rack. The cake will fall in the centre a little. When cold, remove from the tin and turn out onto a plate. Dust with icing sugar.

# ☙ Chocolate Pudding Cake

*1½ cups water*
*1 cup raisins*
*250 g butter*
*1 cup granulated sugar*
*½ teaspoon ground cinnamon*
*½ teaspoon ground ginger*
*½ teaspoon ground mixed spice*
*3 heaped tablespoons cocoa powder*
*pinch of salt*
*1 teaspoon bicarbonate of soda mixed with*
    *¼ cup boiling water*
*2 cups plain flour*

Preheat the oven to 180°C. Line a 23-cm round cake tin
with non-stick baking paper.

   Combine the water, raisins, butter, sugar, spices, cocoa
and salt in a saucepan. Gently heat until boiling; then turn
down to a simmer and cook for 5 minutes. Remove from
the heat and allow to cool. Stir in the bicarbonate of soda
mixture. Fold in the sifted flour to make a smooth cake
batter.

   Pour into the prepared tin and bake for 35–40 minutes
or until firm and cooked through. Cool in the tin before
turning out onto a rack.

   Serve warm with Butterscotch Sauce or Pouring Custard
(see pages 6 and 10).

# ✒ Classic Orange and Almond Cake

*2 whole, thin-skinned oranges*
*6 eggs*
*250 g castor sugar*
*250 g ground almonds*
*1 teaspoon baking powder*

Place the oranges in a saucepan of cold water and cover.
Bring to the boil and cook at a simmer for 2 hours (or
until soft). Cool and blend to a pulp in a food processor.

Preheat the oven to 180°C. Lightly grease a 24-cm round
cake tin and line the base with non-stick baking paper.

Beat the eggs until fluffy adding the sugar slowly until a
thick, pale mousse-like mixture forms. Carefully fold in the
ground almonds and baking powder. Stir in the pulped
oranges.

Pour the batter into the prepared tin and bake for 35–40
minutes or until cooked through. Cool in the tin before
turning out.

Serve with fresh orange slices, chopped dates and plain
creamy yogurt.

## Coconut Cake with Caramel Rum Sauce

*1 cup castor sugar*
*120 g softened butter*
*1 tablespoon vanilla extract*
*2 eggs*
*1 cup self-raising flour*
*¾ cup sour cream*
*¾ cup shredded coconut*
*¼ cup coconut cream*
*2 tablespoons shredded coconut*

Preheat the oven to 175°C. Lightly grease a 22-cm round springform cake tin and line the base with non-stick baking paper.

Cream the sugar, butter and vanilla extract until light and fluffy. Add the eggs, one at a time. Fold in the sifted flour; then stir in the sour cream, shredded coconut and coconut cream. Mix to a smooth batter.

Pour into the prepared tin and sprinkle the shredded coconut over the top. Bake for 45–55 minutes or until lightly browned and cooked through. Cool in the tin on a rack.

Serve with Caramel Rum Sauce (see page 6).

## ⌇ Easy Fruit and Nut Loaf

*175 g softened butter*
*1 cup castor sugar*
*4 eggs*
*3 tablespoons sweet sherry*
*1 teaspoon vanilla extract*
*½ cup chopped dried apricots*
*½ cup chopped dried dates*
*½ cup chopped dried figs*
*½ cup roasted hazelnuts, roughly chopped*
*½ cup pecan nuts, roughly chopped*
*250 g plain flour*
*pinch of salt*

Preheat the oven to 180°C. Lightly butter and flour a
23-cm × 12-cm loaf pan.

Cream the butter and sugar until light and fluffy. Add
the eggs one at a time. Beat in the sweet sherry and vanilla
extract.

Mix the dried fruit and nuts into the sifted flour and add
the pinch of salt. Stir into the egg-and-butter mixture until
combined.

Pour into the prepared pan and bake for 1 hour or until
the cake is golden and cooked through.

Cool in the tin for 15 minutes before turning out onto
a rack.

# ❧ Espresso Coffee and Walnut Cake

*125 g icing sugar*
*4 eggs, separated*
*1 tablespoon fresh breadcrumbs*
*1 tablespoon finely ground espresso coffee beans*
*1 tablespoon cocoa powder*
*180 g walnuts, roughly chopped*
*icing sugar, for dusting*

Preheat the oven to 180°C. Lightly grease a 20-cm round springform cake tin and line the base with non-stick baking paper.

Using an electric mixer beat the icing sugar and egg yolks until pale and thick. Stir in the breadcrumbs, coffee beans, cocoa and walnuts.

In another bowl, whip the egg whites until stiff. Fold two large spoonfuls of the coffee batter into the egg whites. Tip the egg-white mixture into the coffee batter and fold carefully with a spoon.

Pour the batter into the prepared tin and bake for 55–60 minutes or until cooked through. Cool in the tin before carefully turning out onto a serving plate. Dust with icing sugar.

Serve with whipped cream.

# ❧ Fig, Ginger and Pecan Loaf

*185 g softened butter*
*150 g castor sugar*
*3 eggs, lightly beaten*
*150 g sultanas*
*150 g glacé figs*
*150 g glacé ginger*
*75 g plain flour*
*75 g self-raising flour*
*75 g pecan nuts, roughly copped*

Preheat the oven to 160°C. Lightly grease a 23-cm × 12-cm loaf pan and line the base with non-stick baking paper.

Cream the butter and sugar until light and fluffy. Slowly add the eggs until combined. Stir in the sultanas, figs and ginger. Sift the flours into another bowl and mix in the nuts. Fold into the cake batter.

Spoon into the prepared pan and bake for 1¼ hours or until cooked through. Cool in the tin for 20 minutes before turning out onto a rack.

# Ginger and Sour Cream Cake

1½ cups self-raising flour
1½ teaspoons ground ginger
1½ cups brown sugar
3 eggs, lightly beaten
180 g melted butter
125 ml sour cream

Preheat the oven to 180°C. Lightly grease a 23-cm round springform cake tin and line the base with non-stick baking paper.

Sift the flour and ginger into a mixing bowl and stir in the sugar. Stir in the eggs and melted butter. Combine to a smooth batter.

Spoon into the prepared tin and smear the sour cream over the top.

Bake for 45 minutes or until lightly browned on top.

Cool for 10 minutes in the tin on a rack. Turn out onto the rack and cool completely before serving.

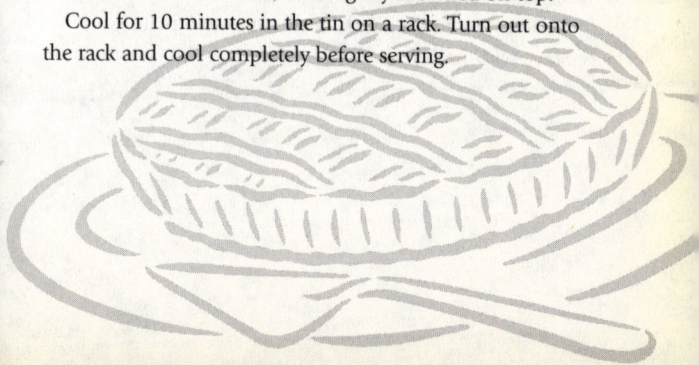

# Greek Hazelnut and Yogurt Cake

*3 large eggs, separated*
*100 g soft brown sugar*
*3 tablespoons Greek-style yogurt*
*grated zest of 1 lemon*
*160 g roasted hazelnuts, ground to a coarse meal in a food*
   *processor*

Preheat the oven to 180°C. Lightly grease a 23-cm round springform cake tin and line the base with non-stick baking paper.

Whisk the egg yolks with the sugar until thick and creamy. Stir in the yogurt, lemon zest and hazelnuts.

In another bowl, whip the egg whites until stiff. Carefully fold the whipped egg whites through the hazelnut mixture.

Spoon into the prepared tin and bake for 35 minutes or until cooked through.

Cool in the tin on a rack. Turn out onto a plate.

Serve with fresh fruit slices.

# Hazelnut, Ricotta and Chocolate Cake

*225 g softened butter*
*250 g castor sugar*
*6 × 60 g eggs, separated*
*60 g plain flour*
*½ cup grated dark chocolate*
*350 g ground roasted hazelnuts*
*400 g ricotta cheese*
*1 teaspoon vanilla essence*

Preheat the oven to 160°C. Grease a 23-cm round cake tin and line the base with non-stick baking paper.

Cream the butter and sugar until light and fluffy. Add the egg yolks one at a time.

Combine the sifted flour, chocolate and hazelnuts and fold into the batter. Stir in the ricotta and vanilla essence. Whisk the egg whites until soft peaks form; then fold into the batter.

Bake for 45–50 minutes or until the cake is cooked through. Cool in the tin before turning out.

## ✒ Italian Polenta, Raisin and Ricotta Cake

*150 g raisins*
*60 ml brandy*
*200 g coarse polenta*
*200 g self-raising flour*
*1 heaped teaspoon baking powder*
*250 g castor sugar*
*250 g ricotta cheese*
*100 g melted butter*
*175 ml warm water*

Preheat the oven to 170°C. Lightly grease a 20-cm round springform cake tin and line the base with non-stick baking paper.

Place the raisins in a saucepan with the brandy and heat gently for 3–4 minutes until plumped up. Set aside to cool.

Combine the polenta, sifted flour and baking powder. Stir in the sugar, ricotta, melted butter and water. Beat, using an electric mixer, until well combined. Stir in the raisins and brandy.

Spoon the mixture into the prepared tin. Bake for 1–1½ hours or until cooked through.

Cool in the tin for 20 minutes; then remove from the tin and cool on a rack.

Serve with whipped cream or mascarpone.

# ❧ Lemon Poppyseed Traybake

*120 g softened butter*
*120 g castor sugar*
*175 g self-raising flour*
*1½ teaspoons baking powder*
*finely grated zest of 1 lemon*
*1 tablespoon poppy seeds*
*2 tablespoons milk*
*2 eggs, lightly beaten*
*100 g castor sugar, dissolved in the juice of 1 lemon*

Preheat the oven to 180°C. Line a 30-cm × 20-cm lamington pan with non-stick baking paper.

Cream the butter and sugar until light and fluffy. Sift the flour and baking powder together and fold into the sugar mixture. Add the lemon zest, poppy seeds, milk and eggs. Mix to a smooth batter.

Pour into the prepared tin and smooth the top.

Bake for 20–25 minutes or until the cake is golden brown and pulls away from the sides of the tin. Brush the lemon syrup over the warm cake.

Allow to cool a little; then turn out onto a rack to cool completely. Cut into 6–8 squares.

## ✄ Lemon Semolina Cake with Orange Glaze

¾ cup self-raising flour
1 teaspoon baking powder
1½ cups semolina
1 cup castor sugar
¾ cup plain creamy yogurt
½ cup buttermilk
½ cup canola oil
3 eggs
grated zest and juice of 1 lemon
½ cup orange marmalade
4 tablespoons orange juice

Preheat the oven to 190°C. Lightly grease a 23-cm round cake tin and line the base with non-stick baking paper.

Sift the flour, baking powder, semolina and sugar into a mixing bowl. In another bowl, combine the yogurt, buttermilk, oil, eggs, and lemon zest and juice. Make a well in the centre and pour the wet mixture into the dry ingredients. Stir to make a runny batter.

Pour into the prepared tin and bake for 35–40 minutes or until lightly browned on top and cooked through. Cool in the tin for 5 minutes before turning out onto a rack.

Heat the marmalade and juice in a saucepan and stir until melted. Pour over the cooled cake and allow to set.

Serve with yogurt mixed with a little honey.

# ❦ Lemony Swiss Roll

*4 large eggs, separated*
*150 g castor sugar*
*125 ml lemon juice*
*grated zest of 2 lemons*
*50 g ground almonds*
*icing sugar, for dusting*

Filling
*125 ml cream*
*4 tablespoons Lemon Curd (see page 8)*
*2 tablespoons toasted flaked almonds*

Preheat the oven to 190°C. Line a 30-cm × 25-cm Swiss roll tin with non-stick baking paper.

Whisk the egg yolks and sugar until thick and creamy. Stir in the lemon juice and zest, and the ground almonds. In another bowl, whip the egg whites until stiff. Carefully fold into the cake batter. Pour into the prepared tin.

Bake for 20–25 minutes or until set and lightly browned. Cool in the tin for 5–8 minutes. Carefully turn the cake out onto a double thickness of greaseproof paper and remove the baking paper. Cover with a tea towel until cool.

Whip the cream until thick and fold in the Lemon Curd and flaked almonds. Spread over the cake and roll up carefully. Place on a serving platter, 'seam' side down, and dust liberally with icing sugar.

## ⌘ Little Christmas Cakes

*875 g sultanas*
*375 g raisins*
*125 g currants*
*125 g mixed peel*
*200 g glacé cherries*
*¾ cup sherry*
*1 tablespoon orange marmalade*
*375 g softened butter*
*1½ cups brown sugar*
*6 eggs*
*3 cups plain flour*
*3 teaspoons mixed spice*

Mix the fruit together with the sherry and marmalade and leave to marinate overnight.

Preheat the oven to 145°C. Lightly grease and line four deep 12-cm square cake tins with a double thickness of non-stick baking paper.

Cream the butter and sugar until light and fluffy. Add the eggs one at a time until well combined. Sift the flour and mixed spice together and stir into the marinated fruit. Fold the butter mixture and fruit mixture together until well combined. Spoon the mixture evenly into the cake tins, smooth the top and push the mixture into the corners evenly. Bake for 2 hours (rotating the cakes every

30 minutes). Cool in the tins for 30 minutes before turning out onto a rack to cool completely.

Tie festive ribbon around the cakes, making a large, attractive bow on the top. Store in an airtight tin until ready to eat or give away as Christmas presents.

# Madeira Cake

*175 g softened butter*
*175 g castor sugar*
*grated zest of 1 lemon*
*225 g plain flour*
*1 teaspoon baking powder*
*3 eggs, lightly beaten*
*2 tablespoons milk*
*3 slices candied citrus peel, cut into small pieces*

Preheat the oven to 180°C. Lightly grease a 20-cm round cake tin and line the base with non-stick baking paper.

Cream the butter, sugar and lemon zest until light and fluffy. Add the sifted flour and baking powder. Slowly add the eggs, alternating with a tablespoon of flour. Fold in the remainder of the flour and then the milk.

Pour into the prepared tin and bake for 1 hour. Sprinkle with the citrus peel and return to the oven. Bake for a further 30 minutes or until lightly browned, risen and cooked through. Cool in the tin for 15 minutes before carefully turning out onto a rack to cool completely.

# 🌱 Marble Cake

*175 g softened butter*
*175 g castor sugar*
*3 eggs, lightly beaten*
*175 g self-raising flour*
*50 g chocolate, melted (keep warm until ready to use)*

Preheat the oven to 180°C. Lightly grease a 20-cm round cake tin and line the base with non-stick baking paper.

Cream the butter and sugar until soft and fluffy. Add the eggs a little at a time until well combined. Stir in the sifted flour. Remove half of the mixture and stir in the melted chocolate until well combined.

Drop spoonfuls of the cake mixtures into the prepared tin, alternating between mixtures and starting with the light mixture. Bake for 1–1¼ hours or until cooked through.

Cool in the tin for 10 minutes before turning out onto a rack to cool completely.

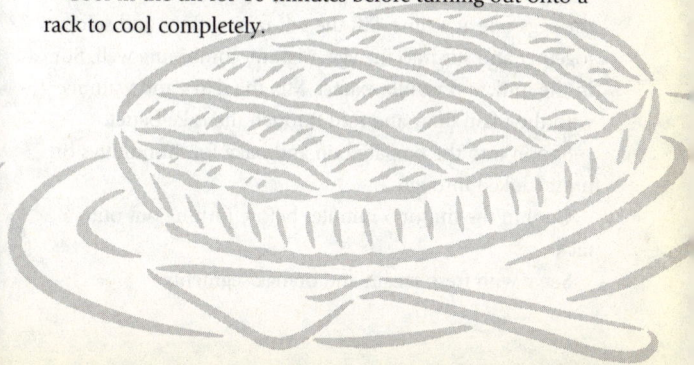

# ☙ Moroccan Date and Walnut Cake

*150 g butter*
*125 g sugar*
*4 eggs*
*1 cup self-raising flour*
*1 teaspoon ground cinnamon*
*1 teaspoon ground nutmeg*
*½ teaspoon ground cloves*
*½ cup milk*
*½ teaspoon pure vanilla extract*
*1 cup pitted chopped dates*
*½ cup chopped walnuts*
*2 tablespoons plain flour*

Preheat the oven to 160°C. Lightly grease a 22-cm round
cake tin and line the base with non-stick baking paper.

Cream the butter and sugar until light and fluffy. Add
the eggs one at a time. Sift the self-raising flour and spices
together and stir into the egg mixture, combining well. Stir
in the milk and vanilla extract. Mix the dates and walnuts
with the plain flour and fold through the cake batter.

Spoon into the prepared tin and bake for 30 minutes or
until cooked through.

Cool in the tin for 5 minutes before turning out onto a
rack.

Serve with fresh cream and orange segments.

# ❦ Nutty Orange and Lemon Cake

*3 eggs, separated*
*³/₄ cup castor sugar*
*grated zest of 1 lemon*
*grated zest of 1 small orange*
*1 teaspoon vanilla essence*
*¹/₂ cup finely ground hazelnuts*
*¹/₂ cup finely ground almonds*
*¹/₂ cup self-raising flour*
*pinch of salt*

Preheat the oven to 170°C. Lightly grease a 23-cm round cake tin and line the base with non-stick baking paper.

Whisk the egg yolks and sugar until thick and creamy (about 3 minutes). Stir in the lemon and orange zest and vanilla essence. Mix the nuts together with the flour and fold into the egg mixture. In another bowl, whip the egg whites with a pinch of salt until stiff. Carefully fold 2 large spoonfuls of egg whites through the nutty cake batter. Tip the cake batter into the egg whites and carefully fold through.

Spoon into the prepared tin and bake for 25–30 minutes or until lightly browned and cooked through. Cool in the tin for 10 minutes before turning out onto a rack.

Serve warm or cold with fresh berries and whipped cream.

## ✿ Old-fashioned Gingerbread

*225 g softened butter*
*1 cup castor sugar*
*3 eggs, lightly beaten*
*1 cup treacle*
*1 cup milk*
*3 cups plain flour*
*1 teaspoon ground cinnamon*
*1 teaspoon grated nutmeg*
*2 teaspoons ground ginger*
*2 teaspoons bicarbonate of soda*

Preheat the oven to 160°C. Lightly grease a 23-cm square cake tin and line the base with non-stick baking paper.

Cream the sugar and butter until light and fluffy. Slowly add the eggs until well combined. Heat the treacle and milk in a saucepan. Remove and cool a little before stirring into the egg-and-butter mixture. Sift the flour, spices and bicarbonate of soda together. Fold into the wet ingredients.

Spoon the cake batter into the prepared tin and bake for 1 hour or until cooked through.

Cool in the tin before turning the cake out onto a rack to cool completely.

# ❦ Orange Iced Chocolate Teacake

*100 g softened butter*
*150 g castor sugar*
*2 large eggs, lightly beaten*
*2 tablespoons cocoa powder dissolved in 2 tablespoons*
  *hot water*
*grated zest of 1 orange*
*100 g self-raising flour*
*2 tablespoons freshly squeezed orange juice*
*Orange Icing (see page 9)*
*3 slices glacé orange, for decoration*

Preheat the oven to 180°C. Lightly grease a 20-cm round
cake tin and line the base with non-stick baking paper.

Cream the butter and sugar until light and fluffy. Slowly
add the eggs until combined. Beat in the cocoa mixture
and orange zest. Fold in the sifted flour and mix in the
orange juice.

Spoon the batter into the prepared tin and bake for
40–45 minutes or until cooked through. Cool in the tin
for 10–15 minutes before turning out onto a rack.

When cold, spread Orange Icing over the sides and
top of the cake using a spatula. Decorate with chopped
glacé oranges.

## ❦ Pear and Prune Cake

*100 g softened butter*
*250 g castor sugar*
*3 large eggs*
*220 g plain flour*
*1 teaspoon ground cinnamon*
*1 teaspoon baking powder*
*⅓ cup milk*
*1 tablespoon brandy*
*2 firm ripe pears, peeled, cored and cut into small chunks*
*100 g pitted prunes, roughly chopped*
*2 tablespoons castor sugar*

Preheat the oven to 180°C. Lightly butter and flour a 20-cm round springform cake tin.

Cream the butter and the 250g sugar until light and fluffy. Add the eggs one at a time until well combined. Sift the flour, cinnamon and baking powder into another bowl. Spoon the flour mixture into the butter mixture, alternating with the milk to form a smooth batter. Stir in the brandy. Fold the pears and prunes into the batter.

Pour into the prepared tin, sprinkle the 2 tablespoons of castor sugar over the top and bake for 45–55 minutes or until the cake is cooked through. Cool in the tin on a rack.

Turn out and serve with ice-cream or whipped cream.

# ✒ Pear, Chocolate and Almond Traybake

*125 g butter*
*200 g dark chocolate, broken into small pieces*
*3 eggs*
*1 cup castor sugar*
*1 cup self-raising flour*
*1 cup ground almonds*
*2 large Beurre Bosc pears, peeled, cored and thinly sliced*

Preheat the oven to 180°C. Line a 28-cm × 18-cm lamington pan with non-stick baking paper.

Melt the butter in a saucepan over a medium heat. Remove and stir in the chocolate until melted.

Beat the eggs and sugar until pale and thick. Slowly pour in the chocolate mixture and stir gently to combine. Carefully fold in the sifted flour and almonds. Pour the batter into the prepared pan. Arrange the pear slices over the top of the batter.

Bake for 40–45 minutes or until firm and cooked through.

Cool on a rack. Cut into slices and serve with custard or thick cream.

## ✒ Pineapple Blitztorte

110 g softened butter
85 g castor sugar
4 large eggs, separated
2 tablespoons milk
110 g plain flour
1 level teaspoon baking powder
140 g castor sugar
30 g flaked almonds
2 teaspoons castor sugar mixed with ½ teaspoon
    ground cinnamon

Filling
200 g sweet fresh pineapple, peeled, cored and finely chopped
250 ml cream, whipped with
1 teaspoon sugar until fluffy

Preheat the oven to 175°C. Lightly butter and flour two
22-cm round cake tins and line the bases with non-stick
baking paper.

Cream the butter and sugar until light and fluffy.
Add the egg yolks and milk. Sift the flour and baking
powder and stir into the batter. Spoon evenly into the
prepared tins.

Whip the egg whites until stiff; then whisk in the 140 g sugar until thick and glossy.

Spread over the cake batters. Scatter the flaked almonds over the top and sprinkle with cinnamon sugar.

Bake for 30 minutes or until the meringue is lightly browned. Cool in the tins before filling.

Turn one cake out onto a plate with the meringue side down. Spread the cream over the cake and sprinkle with chopped pineapple. Place the other cake on top, with the meringue side up, and serve.

# ❧ Plum Kuchen

1½ cups plain flour
1½ teaspoons baking powder
1 teaspoon ground cinnamon
pinch of salt
100 g softened butter
⅔ cup castor sugar
2 large eggs
2 teaspoons vanilla extract
½ teaspoon almond extract
½ cup sour cream
5 large plums, stones removed and each one cut into 8 slices
¼ cup castor sugar
½ teaspoon ground cinnamon
2 tablespoons melted butter

Preheat the oven to 175°C. Line a 32-cm × 23-cm cake tin
with non-stick baking paper.

Sift the dry ingredients into a bowl. In another bowl,
cream the softened butter and ⅔ cup of sugar until light
and fluffy. Beat in the eggs one at a time, then stir in the
vanilla and almond extracts. Stir in the dry ingredients,
alternating with the sour cream, to make a smooth batter.
Spread into the prepared tin and arrange the plum slices in
4 rows on top.

Mix the ¼ cup of sugar and ½ teaspoon of cinnamon together and sprinkle over the plums. Drizzle with the melted butter.

Bake for 40 minutes or until firm and springy to the touch.

Cool for at least 30 minutes before cutting and serving.

# ❧ Rhubarb and Lemon Cake

*1 cup castor sugar*
*finely grated zest of 2 lemons*
*4 eggs, lightly beaten*
*3 tablespoons milk*
*1³/₄ cups self-raising flour*
*1 tablespoon fresh lemon juice*
*140 g melted butter*
*²/₃ cup light olive oil*
*300 g fresh rhubarb, leaves removed and stalks chopped into*
*    small chunks*

Preheat the oven to 180°C. Line a 26-cm round springform
cake tin with non-stick baking paper, and lightly butter and
flour the sides.

   Using an electric mixer, blend the sugar with the lemon
zest for 1 minute. Add the eggs and beat until pale and
thick (about 3 minutes).

   Stir in the milk and sifted flour to make a smooth batter.
Blend in the lemon juice, melted butter and oil.

   Pour one-third of the batter into the prepared tin,
making sure the base is covered. Arrange the rhubarb over
the top; then pour the rest of the batter over the rhubarb.

   Bake for 50 minutes or until the cake pulls away from
the sides of the tin. Cool for 10 minutes before turning out
onto a rack.

# ✒ Rich Chocolate and Date Cake

*250 g whole unblanched almonds*
*250 g dark cooking chocolate, broken into small pieces*
*250 g pitted dates, roughly chopped*
*6 large egg whites*
*pinch of salt*
*½ cup castor sugar*

Preheat the oven to 180°C. Lightly grease a 23-cm round springform cake tin and line the base with non-stick baking paper.

Chop the nuts and chocolate together using a food processor. Transfer to a mixing bowl and stir in the chopped dates. In another bowl, whisk the egg whites with the pinch of salt until soft peaks form. Slowly whisk in the sugar until thick and glossy. Fold the chocolate mixture through the meringue.

Pour into the prepared tin and bake for 45 minutes or until firm. Cool in the tin; then carefully turn out onto a platter.

Cut into thin wedges and serve with fresh fruit slices and cream.

# ❧ Rich Food Processor Chocolate Cake

1¼ cups plain flour
1½ teaspoons baking powder
¾ teaspoon baking soda
pinch of salt
100 g dark chocolate, broken into small pieces
1½ cups castor sugar
½ cup boiling water
3 large eggs, lightly beaten
1 heaped tablespoon cocoa
225 g softened butter, cut into 8 pieces
¾ cup sour cream
1 tablespoon dark rum

Preheat the oven to 170°C. Grease a 23-cm round springform cake tin and line the base with non-stick baking paper.

Blend the sifted flour, baking powder, baking soda and salt in a food processor for 3 seconds. Remove and reserve.

Process the chocolate and half of the sugar until the mixture resembles fine breadcrumbs.

With the machine running, pour in the boiling water and process until the chocolate has melted. Pour in the eggs, cocoa and remaining sugar. Process for 2 minutes. Add in the butter and process for 1 minute. Add the sour cream and rum.

Spoon the flour into the food processor. Pulse the mixture 3 or 4 times until the flour is incorporated. Be careful not to over-process.

Spoon the mixture into the prepared tin. Bake for 1 hour and 15 minutes or until cooked through. Cool in the tin for 10 minutes before turning out onto a rack.

# ❧ Roasted Pecan and Ginger Cake

*130 g softened butter*
*1 cup brown sugar*
*2 eggs, lightly beaten*
*1 cup plain flour*
*½ tablespoon baking powder*
*2 teaspoons ground ginger*
*⅔ cup roasted pecans, finely chopped*
*⅔ cup milk*
*½ teaspoon fresh grated ginger*
*½ teaspoon vanilla extract*
*10 pecan halves, for decoration*

Preheat the oven to 180°C. Lightly grease a 22-cm round cake tin and line the base with non-stick baking paper.

Cream the butter and sugar until light and fluffy. Slowly add the eggs. Sift the flour, baking powder and ground ginger into another bowl and stir in the pecans. Add the flour mixture to the butter mixture a little at a time, alternating with the milk and finishing with the flour mixture. Stir in the fresh ginger and vanilla extract.

Pour into the prepared tin and decorate the top with the pecan halves.

Bake for 35–40 minutes or until lightly browned and cooked through. Cool on a rack for 10 minutes before turning out of the tin to cool completely.

# ☙ Rum and Lime Glazed Banana Bread

¾ *cup soft brown sugar*
*120 g softened butter*
*2 eggs, lightly beaten*
*1 cup mashed ripe bananas (about 3)*
*3 tablespoons buttermilk*
*1 tablespoon fresh lime juice*
½ *teaspoon salt*
½ *teaspoon ground ginger*
*2 cups self-raising flour*
½ *teaspoon bicarbonate of soda*

Glaze
¼ *cup soft brown sugar*
*1 tablespoon rum*
*20 g butter*
*3 tablespoons fresh lime juice*

Preheat the oven to 175°C. Lightly grease a 25-cm × 15-cm loaf pan.

Cream the sugar and butter until light and fluffy. Stir in the eggs, bananas, buttermilk and lime juice and combine. Sift the salt, ginger and flour into a mixing bowl with the bicarbonate of soda. Stir into the cake batter and combine until smooth. Spoon into the prepared pan and bake for 1 hour. Allow the cake to stand for 10 minutes before turning out onto a rack.

>

Meanwhile, heat all the glaze ingredients in a saucepan. Stir for about 5 minutes to form a smooth syrup.

Coat the top and sides of the cake with the glaze. Serve while warm or at room temperature.

# 🌿 Seed Cake

*125 g softened butter*
*125 g castor sugar*
*2 eggs, beaten*
*125 g self-raising flour*
*½ teaspoon baking powder*
*50 g ground almonds*
*2 heaped teaspoons caraway seeds*
*3 tablespoons plain yogurt*
*4 teaspoons toasted rolled oats*
*icing sugar, for dusting*

Preheat the oven to 180°C. Lightly grease a 20-cm round cake tin and line the base with non-stick baking paper.

Cream the butter and sugar until light and fluffy. Slowly add the eggs until well combined. Sift the flour and baking powder into another bowl. Stir in the almonds and caraway seeds. Fold into the butter mixture and stir in the yogurt.

Spoon into the prepared tin, sprinkle with toasted rolled oats and dust with icing sugar.

Bake for 45 minutes–1 hour or until the cake is cooked through. Cool in the tin for 10 minutes before turning out onto a rack to cool completely.

# Strawberry Shortcake

*225 g self-raising flour*
*1/2 teaspoon baking powder*
*good pinch of salt*
*75 g softened butter*
*150 g castor sugar*
*1 medium egg, beaten*
*1/4 cup buttermilk*
*icing sugar, for dusting*

Filling
*250 g strawberries, stalks removed, cut in half and mixed*
   *with 1 dessertspoon castor sugar*
*200 ml fresh cream, whipped until thick*

Preheat the oven to 190°C. Lightly grease two 20-cm round
cake tins and line the bases with non-stick baking paper.

Combine the sifted flour, baking powder and salt in a
large mixing bowl. Add the butter and rub into the flour
until the mixture resembles coarse breadcrumbs. Mix in the
sugar and the egg; then stir in enough buttermilk to form a
soft dough. Divide into two and, with floured hands, press
lightly into the tins.

Bake for 20–25 minutes or until firm and lightly
browned. Turn out on a rack to cool.

Fill with strawberries and whipped cream, and dust with
icing sugar.

# ✒ Streusel Pumpkin Cake

$^1/_3$ cup castor sugar
60 g softened butter
$^1/_3$ cup cooked mashed pumpkin
$^1/_4$ cup sour cream
1 egg, lightly beaten
$1^1/_4$ cups plain flour
$^1/_4$ teaspoon grated nutmeg
1 tablespoon baking powder
$^1/_2$ teaspoon bicarbonate of soda
$^1/_3$ cup orange juice
2 teaspoons grated orange zest

Streusel Topping
$^1/_4$ cup brown sugar
45 g chilled butter, cut into small pieces
2 tablespoons plain flour
$^1/_2$ teaspoon ground cinnamon
$^1/_3$ cup pecans, roughly chopped

Preheat the oven to 180°C. Lightly grease a 22-cm round springform cake tin and line the base with non-stick baking paper.

Beat the sugar, butter, pumpkin, sour cream and egg until well combined.

Sift the flour, nutmeg, baking powder and bicarbonate of soda into another bowl. Make a well in the centre and    >

stir in the pumpkin mixture and orange juice, alternating
between the two, until well combined. Stir in the orange
zest.

Pour the batter into the prepared tin.

Combine the Streusel Topping ingredients in a bowl
until the mixture resembles coarse breadcrumbs. Sprinkle
the mixture over the cake batter.

Bake for 45 minutes or until firm and cooked through.
Cool in the tin; then turn out onto a rack.

Serve warm or cold with thickened cream or yogurt.

# ✌ Syd's Lamingtons

150 g softened butter
150 g castor sugar
2 eggs
½ teaspoon vanilla essence
4 tablespoons milk
275 g self-raising flour
200 g desiccated coconut, for decoration

Icing
3 tablespoons cocoa
3 tablespoons drinking chocolate
3 tablespoons water
3 tablespoons castor sugar
30 g butter

Preheat the oven to 180°C. Line a 25-cm × 20-cm
lamington pan with non-stick baking paper.

Cream the butter and sugar until light and fluffy.
In another bowl, beat the eggs, vanilla essence and milk.
Slowly beat this mixture into the butter mixture. Fold in
the sifted flour and add more milk if necessary to form a
smooth batter.

Pour into the prepared pan and bake for 30 minutes or
until golden. Cool for 5 minutes before turning out onto
a rack to cool completely.

Meanwhile, stir all the icing ingredients in a saucepan over a gentle heat, for 5–6 minutes, until the mixture is smooth and glossy. Remove and cool a little.

When the cake is completely cold, cut into 20 squares. Using tongs or piercing the cake with a metal skewer, dip each square into the icing to completely cover it, then roll in the coconut. Continue until all the cakes have been iced and covered with coconut.

# ✥ Traditional Baked Cheesecake

Base
*50 g rolled oats*
*100 g sweet biscuit crumbs*
*75 g melted butter*

Filling
*3 eggs, separated*
*150 g castor sugar*
*300 g cream cheese*
*1 tablespoon plain flour*
*grated zest and juice of 1 lemon*
*50 g sultanas*
*100 ml sour cream*

Preheat the oven to 170°C. Lightly grease a 20-cm spring-form cake tin and line the base with non-stick baking paper.

Combine the base ingredients and press into the base of the prepared tin. Refrigerate while you make the filling.

Whisk the egg yolks together with the sugar until thick and creamy. Beat in the cream cheese, sifted flour, zest and juice. Fold in the sultanas and the sour cream. Whip the egg whites until stiff; then carefully fold them through the egg-yolk mixture. Pour into the prepared tin and bake for 1 hour or until firm to the touch. Cool completely before serving with orange segments and chopped strawberries.

## ✌ Treacle, Prune and Walnut Loaf

*175 g self-raising flour*
*175 g plain wholemeal flour*
*½ teaspoon salt*
*½ teaspoon bicarbonate of soda*
*50 g walnuts, roughly chopped*
*75 g stoned prunes, roughly chopped*
*275 mls buttermilk*
*2 tablespoons treacle*

Preheat the oven to 200°C. Lightly grease and line a
25-cm × 15-cm loaf pan with non-stick baking paper.

Sift the flours into a mixing bowl with the salt and
bicarbonate of soda. Mix in the walnuts and prunes.

Warm the buttermilk in a saucepan and stir in the treacle
until the treacle has dissolved. Make a well in the centre of
the flour mixture and stir in the buttermilk mixture. Fold
quickly to make a soft dough.

Pour into the loaf pan and bake for 30–35 minutes or
until firm and cooked through. Cool in the tin; then turn
out onto a rack.

Delicious served with cheddar cheese or a salty blue
cheese.

# ☙ Vintage Victoria Sponge Cake with Cream and Jam

*225 g softened butter*
*225 g castor sugar*
*4 eggs*
*225 g self-raising flour*
*2 teaspoons baking powder*
*¼ cup strawberry or raspberry jam*
*150 ml thickened cream, whipped until thick*
*icing sugar, for dusting*

Preheat the oven to 180°C. Lightly grease two 20-cm sandwich cake tins and line the bases with non-stick baking paper.

Combine the butter, sugar, eggs, sifted flour and baking powder and beat until well blended and thoroughly mixed to a creamy cake batter. Divide the mixture between the two cake tins.

Bake for 25–30 minutes or until lightly browned and cooked through.

Cool in the tin for 10 minutes. Turn out onto a rack to cool completely.

Fill with jam and cream and dust with icing sugar.

# Walnut Fudge Cake

*³/₄ cup brown sugar*
*150 g butter*
*100 g dark chocolate*
*¹/₂ cup condensed milk*
*2 cups chopped walnuts*
*³/₄ cup self-raising flour*
*¹/₄ cup milk*
*1 egg, lightly beaten*
*icing sugar, for dusting*

Preheat the oven to 180°C. Lightly grease a 20-cm round cake tin and line the base with non-stick baking paper.

Heat the sugar, butter, chocolate, condensed milk and walnuts in a saucepan, stirring over a low heat until the mixture has thickened and the sugar is dissolved.

Remove from the heat and cool a little. Pour into a mixing bowl. Stir in the sifted flour, milk and egg until well combined. Spoon into the prepared tin and smooth the top.

Bake for 30–40 minutes or until cooked through but still moist in the middle.

Cool in the tin before cutting and dusting with icing sugar.

Serve with ice-cream.

# Whisked Sponge Cake with Coffee Icing

*3 large eggs*
*125 g castor sugar*
*85 g self-raising flour*
*Coffee Icing (see page 7)*
*½ cup chocolate-coated coffee beans, for decoration*

Preheat the oven to 190°C. Lightly grease a 20-cm round cake tin and line the base with non-stick baking paper.

Beat the eggs and sugar until pale and thick. Sift the flour into the mixture and carefully fold through.

Pour into the cake tin and bake for 30–35 minutes or until firm and cooked through.

Turn out onto a rack to cool. When cold, cut in half horizontally. Carefully, using a spatula, spread about one-third of the Coffee Icing as a filling for the cake. Spread the rest of the icing to cover the whole cake. Decorate with chocolate-coated coffee beans around the top and sides.

# PUDDINGS

# Apple and Orange Pudding

## Serves 4

*1 kg Granny Smith apples, peeled, cored and cut into chunks*
*grated zest and juice of 1 orange*
*50 g soft brown sugar*

*Topping*
*100 g softened butter*
*100 g soft brown sugar*
*2 large eggs*
*1 teaspoon baking powder*
*150 g self-raising flour, sifted*
*50 g flaked almonds, for decoration*

Preheat the oven to 180°C. Lightly grease a 2-litre ovenproof dish.

Combine the apples, orange zest and juice, and brown sugar in the ovenproof dish. Place all the topping ingredients in an electric mixer and beat slowly until combined. Beat on high speed until soft and fluffy (about 1 minute).

Spoon the topping over the apples to cover them, spreading the mixture to the edges. Sprinkle the flaked almonds over the top.

Bake for 35–40 minutes or until lightly browned on top. Serve immediately with ice-cream or cream.

# 🥧 Apple, Blackberry and Rhubarb Blanket Pie

Serves 6

Pastry
*200 g plain flour*
*125 g butter, cut into small pieces*
*4–5 tablespoons sour cream or chilled water*
*2 tablespoons milk or egg wash for glazing the pastry*
*1 tablespoon castor sugar*

Filling
*400 g rhubarb, trimmed and cut into small chunks*
*250 g apples, cored, peeled and cut into small chunks*
*250 g fresh blackberries or mulberries (or use defrosted frozen berries)*
*100 g castor sugar*

Preheat the oven to 200°C. Lightly flour a shallow baking tin or pizza tray.

Sift the flour into a food processor and add the butter. Process for 1 minute or until the mixture resembles coarse breadcrumbs. Add the sour cream or chilled water and pulse until the pastry dough comes together. Remove and shape into a ball. Chill for 20 minutes while you prepare the filling.

>

Mix all the fruit together in a bowl and stir in the sugar. Working on a floured board, roll out the pastry to about 30 cm in diameter. Using a rolling pin, lift the pastry onto the prepared tin or tray. Spoon the fruit into the middle and carefully bring the pastry up, folding it to make a round free-form shape. Leave a small gap in the centre, exposing some of the fruit.

Brush the pastry with milk and sprinkle over the castor sugar.

Bake for 30–40 minutes or until the pastry is crisp and golden and the fruit is tender. Cool a little before lifting onto a serving plate.

Serve warm with Pouring Custard (see page 10).

# ✒ Baked Egg Custard

## Serves 6

*4 eggs*
*500 ml milk or cream or half and half*
*1 teaspoon vanilla essence*
*1 teaspoon grated zest of orange*
*3 tablespoons brown sugar*
*pinch of ground nutmeg*
*500 g dark raisins*

Preheat the oven to 180°C. Lightly grease a 1-litre
ovenproof dish or 6 individual ramekin dishes.

Whisk the eggs and milk lightly and stir in the vanilla
essence, orange zest, brown sugar and nutmeg.

Sprinkle the raisins over the bottom of the prepared
dish(es) and pour the egg mixture over the top. Place the
dish(es) into a bain marie (see page 4).

If using a 1-litre dish, bake for 40–60 minutes or until
just set. Adjust the time to 25–30 minutes for individual
dishes.

Cool a little before serving.

Delicious served with poached seasonal fruit.

# Baked Rice Pudding with Lemon

## Serves 6

*1/3 cup short-grain rice*
*1/2 cup castor sugar*
*1 litre milk*
*25 g butter*
*finely grated zest of 1 lemon*

Preheat the oven to 175°C. Grease a 2-litre ovenproof dish.
   Sprinkle the rice over the bottom of the prepared dish.
Combine the sugar and milk and pour over the rice.
Dot the top with butter.
   Bake for 1 hour. Stir in the lemon zest and bake for a
further 15–20 minutes. Allow to stand for 10 minutes.
   Serve warm with a little pouring cream.

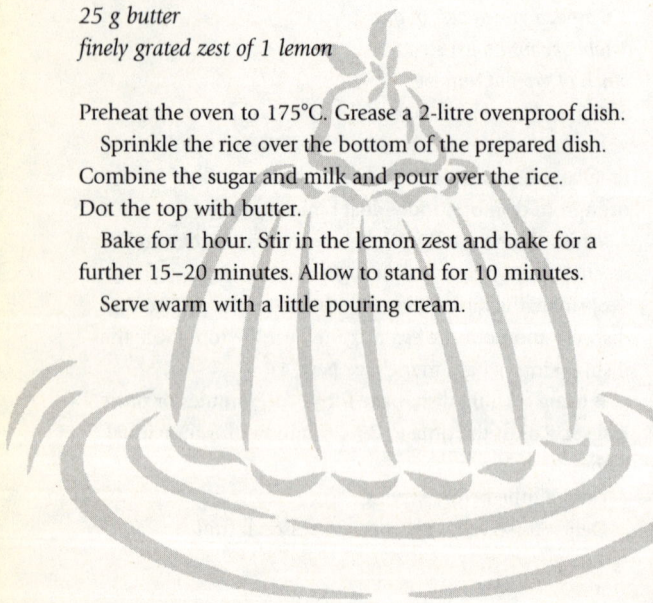

# ✍ Baked Roly Poly with Hot Jam Sauce

Serves 6

1½ cups self-raising flour
½ cup plain flour
60 g softened butter
¾ cup buttermilk
6 tablespoons strawberry jam

Hot Jam Sauce
3 tablespoons blackberry jam
finely grated zest and juice of 1 large orange

Preheat the oven to 175°C. Lightly grease a shallow baking dish.

Sift the flours into a mixing bowl. Add the butter and rub together until the mixture resembles fine breadcrumbs. Slowly pour in the buttermilk until the mixture comes together and forms a sticky dough.

On a floured board, roll out the dough to approximately 25 cm × 20 cm. Spread the jam over the dough, leaving a border around the edges. Roll up evenly from the short side. Wrap the roll in non-stick baking paper and place in the prepared dish. Bake for 40–45 minutes or until golden.

To make the sauce heat the jam, orange zest and juice together over a gentle heat until well combined. Spoon over the roly poly and serve immediately.

## ✑ Baked Stuffed Apples

### Serves 6

*6 large Granny Smith or Golden Delicious apples*
*25 g butter*
*25 g soft brown sugar*
*100 ml white wine or sherry*

*Filling*
*175 g dried dates, roughly chopped*
*75 g walnuts, roughly chopped*
*grated zest and juice of 1 lemon*

Preheat the oven to 190°C. Lightly grease a shallow baking dish.

Core the apples and score the skin around the middle of each one.

Combine the dates, nuts and lemon zest and juice.

Spoon the filling into the apple cavities and place the apples into the prepared dish. Place a little butter on top of each apple and sprinkle with brown sugar. Pour in the wine or sherry.

Bake for about 1 hour, basting with a little of the juices.

Serve warm or cold with whipped cream.

# ✈ Baked Stuffed Peaches

## Serves 6

¾ cup ground almonds
6 amaretti biscuits (almond macaroons), crushed
2 tablespoons castor sugar
1 large egg, lightly beaten
½ cup ricotta cheese
6 large, ripe, firm peaches, cut in half and stones removed
½ cup white wine
¼ cup orange juice
25 g butter

Preheat the oven to 180°C. Lightly grease a shallow
ovenproof dish.

Combine the almonds, crushed macaroons and sugar.
Stir in the egg and ricotta cheese. Mix to form a sticky ball.
Spoon into the cavities of the halved peaches.

Place in the prepared dish and pour the wine and orange
juice over the top. Dot the top of each peach with butter.

Bake for 25–30 minutes or until lightly browned on top.

Serve warm or cold with ice-cream or Pouring Custard
(see page 10).

# ❧ Banana and Fresh Fig Gratin

## Serves 4

*4 fresh figs, quartered*
*4 ripe, firm bananas, peeled and thickly sliced*
*3 eggs*
*1½ tablespoons ground almonds*
*1 teaspoon vanilla extract*
*300 ml cream*
*¼ cup brown sugar*
*icing sugar, for dusting*

Preheat the oven to 180°C. Lightly grease a shallow baking dish and place the fruit in the bottom.

Beat the eggs, almonds, vanilla extract, cream and brown sugar. Pour over the fruit.

Place on a preheated baking tray and bake for 10–15 minutes or until nearly set.

Place under a hot grill until lightly browned.

Dust liberally with icing sugar before serving warm.

# 🍋 Banana Bread Pudding

## Serves 8

½ cup orange marmalade
5 thick slices white bread
3 large bananas, peeled and cut into thick slices
4 large eggs, lightly beaten
1 litre milk
2 cups sugar
1 tablespoon vanilla extract
1 teaspoon ground nutmeg
1 tablespoon ground cinnamon
4 tablespoons melted butter
icing sugar, for dusting

Preheat the oven to 180°C. Lightly grease a 2-litre
ovenproof dish.

Spread the marmalade over the bread slices; then cut the
bread into small chunks. Lay half of the bread chunks over
the base of the prepared dish. Arrange the banana slices
over the bread; then place the remainder of the bread
chunks on the top.

Combine the eggs, milk, sugar, vanilla extract and spices.
Whisk in the melted butter. Pour the mixture over the
bread and bananas.

>

Cover the dish with foil and place into a bain marie (see page 4). Bake for 30 minutes. Remove the foil and bake for a further 30 minutes or until the pudding is firm and lightly browned on top.

Remove from the baking dish and cool a little.

Dust with icing sugar before serving.

# 🌿 Banana Mousse Pie

## Serves 6

### Pastry
100 g very cold butter
225 g plain flour
1 teaspoon grated lemon zest
50 g icing sugar
1 egg, lightly beaten
2–3 tablespoons very cold water

### Filling
6 ripe bananas, peeled
½ cup brown sugar
2 tablespoons rum
3 eggs, separated
½ cup flaked almonds
2 tablespoons castor sugar
2 tablespoons icing sugar

Pulse the butter and flour in a food processor until the mixture resembles fine breadcrumbs. Add the lemon zest and icing sugar and pulse for 1 minute.

Combine the egg and water and, with the motor running, slowly pour enough liquid into the food processor to draw the mixture together. Remove and roll into a ball. Chill for 30 minutes.

Preheat the oven to 200°C. Lightly grease a 20-cm pie dish.

On a floured board, roll out the pastry and fit into the prepared dish, cutting away any excess. Blind bake the pastry shell (see page 4) on a preheated baking tray for 10–15 minutes or until lightly browned at the sides.

Reduce the oven temperature to 175°C.

In a food processor, blend 4 of the bananas with the brown sugar, rum and egg yolks until smooth. Whip the egg whites until stiff. Carefully fold through the banana mixture. Pour into the prebaked pastry case. Slice the remaining two bananas over the top of the pie and bake for 20 minutes or until firm.

Sprinkle with almonds and castor sugar.

Preheat the grill until hot and grill the pie for 2–3 minutes to caramelise the nutty topping.

Serve warm or cold dusted with icing sugar.

# ✑ Blackberry and Nectarine Cobbler

### Serves 6

*500 g fresh nectarines, stones removed*
*100 g fresh (or defrosted frozen) blackberries*
*50 g of soft brown sugar*
*grated zest and juice of 1 lemon*

Scone topping
*2 cups plain flour*
*1 tablespoon baking powder*
*pinch of salt*
*125 g butter, cut into small pieces*
*¾ cup very cold milk*
*1 tablespoon melted butter, mixed with*
*2 teaspoons ground cinnamon*

Preheat the oven to 200°C. Lightly grease a 900-ml
ovenproof dish.

Place the nectarines and blackberries into the prepared
dish and sprinkle with sugar, lemon zest and juice.

Sift the flour, baking powder and salt into a mixing
bowl. Add the butter and rub into the flour until mixture
resembles fine breadcrumbs.

Make a well in the centre and pour in the milk, mixing
to form a soft dough. Knead lightly and refrigerate for
20 minutes.

On a floured surface, roll out the dough to a thickness of about 1 cm. Use a scone cutter to cut out enough rounds to completely cover the fruit.

Brush with the melted butter and cinnamon; then bake for 20 minutes. Reduce the oven temperature to 180°C and bake for a further 15 minutes or until lightly browned on top.

Cool a little before serving with ice-cream or Pouring Custard (see page 10).

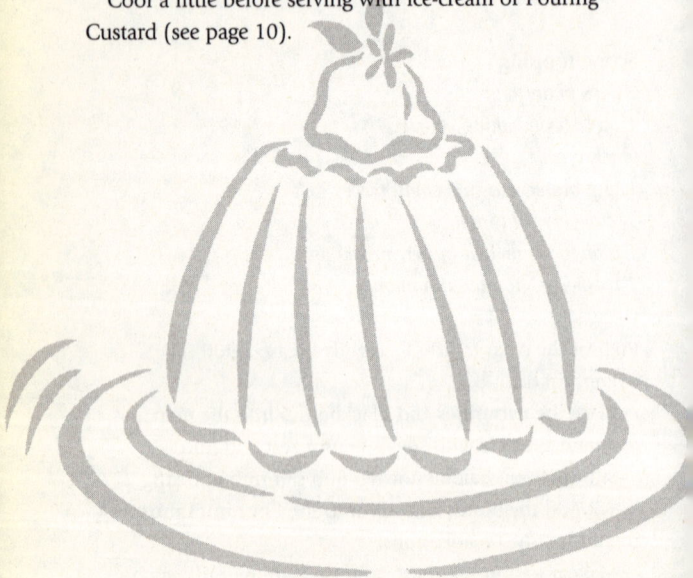

# Chilled Summer Berry Pudding

## Serves 8

1 kg mixed fresh or frozen berries (stoned cherries,
  raspberries, blueberries, blackberries, strawberries,
  mulberries)
225 g castor sugar
100 ml fresh orange juice
10–12 thin slices of white, day-old bread, crusts removed

Combine the fruit, sugar and orange juice in a saucepan.
Cook over a gentle heat for 4–5 minutes or until the sugar
has melted and the fruit juices start to flow. Remove and
cool a little.

Line a 1.7-litre pudding basin with the sliced bread,
cutting it to neatly fit the sides and base. Spoon in about
two-thirds of the fruit, and leave for 30 minutes. Spoon in
the rest of the fruit and cover the top with bread slices so
that the fruit is completely enclosed. Place a piece of cling
wrap or non-stick baking paper over the top; then place a
plate on top of the pudding to weigh it down. Refrigerate
overnight.

Remove the plate and loosen the sides with a palate
knife before turning the pudding out onto a deep-sided
serving plate, to catch any excess fruit juices.

Serve in slices with ice-cream or pouring cream.

# ✌ Chocolate and Walnut Caramel Custard Pudding

## Serves 8

*1 cup granulated sugar*
*¹⁄₃ cup water*
*30 g chocolate*
*³⁄₄ cup toasted walnuts*
*415-g can sweetened condensed milk*
*425 ml milk*
*2 whole eggs, plus 2 egg yolks*
*a little grated chocolate*

Preheat the oven to 175°C. Lightly grease 8 × 125-ml custard cups.

Combine the sugar and water in a small saucepan stirring continually until the sugar dissolves. Increase the heat and boil until the sugar syrup starts to turn a golden brown. Immediately remove from the heat and spoon the caramel evenly into 8 custard cups.

Process the chocolate and walnuts in a food processor for 1–2 minutes. Transfer to a mixing bowl. Heat the condensed milk and milk in a saucepan until boiling. Pour over the chocolate and nuts. Stir until smooth. Cool slightly; then stir in the whole eggs and egg yolks.

Spoon the chocolate mixture evenly into the 8 cups. Place the cups in a bain marie (see page 4). Bake for 45 minutes or until the puddings are just set. Take out of the baking dish. Cool on a rack. Run a knife around the edge of the custards and turn out onto serving plates.

Decorate with grated chocolate.

# ✌ Chocolate Cherry Clafoutis

## Serves 4

*4 tablespoons brandy or rum*
*450 g black cherries, stoned*
*75 g plain flour*
*2 tablespoons cocoa powder*
*pinch of salt*
*50 g icing sugar*
*25 g melted butter*
*300 ml milk*
*3 eggs, lightly beaten*
*icing sugar, for dusting*

Preheat the oven to 220°C. Generously grease a 1-litre ovenproof dish.

Soak the cherries in the brandy or rum for 20 minutes.

Make the batter in a food processor by first sifting the flour, cocoa, salt and icing sugar together. With the motor running, pour in the melted butter, milk and eggs and blend to a smooth batter.

Pour about ½ cup of the batter into the base of the prepared dish and bake for 10 minutes or until just set.

Drain any liquid from the cherries and mix it into the reserved batter. Spoon the cherries over the base of the baking dish; then pour the rest of the batter over the fruit.

Bake for 40–45 minutes or until risen and set. Leave to cool for 5 minutes; then dust generously with icing sugar.

Serve warm with cream or ice-cream.

# ℘ Classic Sponge Pudding with Strawberry Jam Sauce

## Serves 4

*100 g softened butter*
*100 g castor sugar*
*2 eggs, beaten*
*175 g self-raising flour*
*1 teaspoon vanilla extract*
*3–4 tablespoons milk*

Strawberry Jam Sauce
*100 g strawberry jam*
*2 tablespoons castor sugar*
*juice of 1 lemon*
*2 tablespoons water*

Preheat the oven to 190°C, or fill a steaming pan with water. Lightly butter a 900-ml pudding basin or 4 × 200-ml ramekins.

Cream the butter and sugar until light and fluffy. Slowly add the eggs. Fold in the sifted flour, vanilla and milk to make a soft batter that drops off the spoon easily.

Pour into the prepared pudding basin and place in a bain marie (see page 4). Cover tightly with a double thickness of buttered foil, pleated in the centre to allow for expansion of the mixture.

Bake for 1–1½ hours. Alternatively, cook in a steamer on top of the stove for 1½ hours, topping up with water as necessary. Reduce the cooking time to 35–45 minutes for the individual puddings. Remove and turn out.

To make the sauce, place all the ingredients in a saucepan and stir over a gentle heat until smooth. Bring to the boil and cook for 2 minutes. Strain into a jug, and serve with the pudding.

# Coconut Pudding with Passionfruit Sauce

## Serves 6

*4 large eggs*
*finely grated zest and juice of 2 lemons*
*200 g castor sugar*
*375 ml buttermilk*
*1 cup desiccated coconut*

Preheat the oven to 160°C. Lightly grease a 1-litre ovenproof dish.

Combine the eggs, lemon zest and juice, castor sugar, buttermilk and desiccated coconut. Pour into the prepared dish and bake for 45 minutes–1 hour or until firm and lightly golden. Cool completely and serve with Passionfruit Sauce (see page 10) poured over the top.

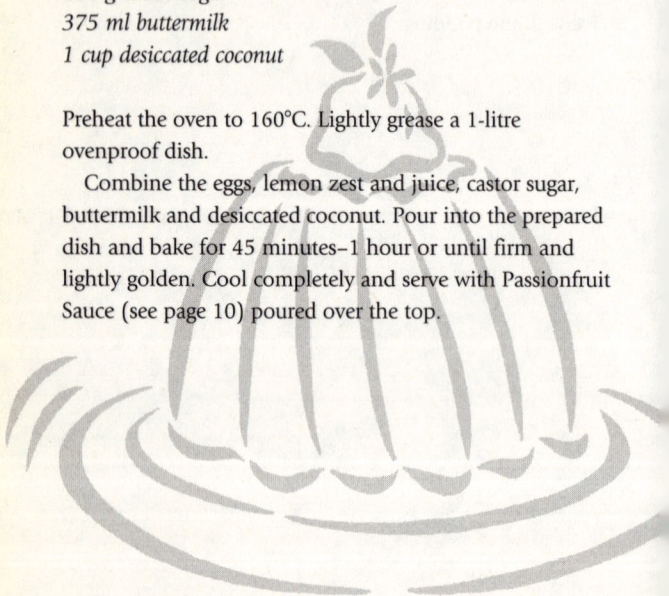

# ✒ Easy Cherry and Ricotta Cheese Strudel

Serves 6

*500 g ricotta cheese*
*2 eggs, lightly beaten*
*¹/₂ cup pitted tinned cherries, well drained*
*50 g soft cream cheese*
*¹/₂ cup dried breadcrumbs*
*3 tablespoons castor sugar*
*4 sheets filo pastry*
*¹/₄ cup melted butter*
*icing sugar, for dusting*

Preheat the oven to 200°C.

Combine the ricotta, eggs, cherries, cream cheese, dried breadcrumbs and sugar. Chill until ready to use.

Place a sheet of non-stick baking paper on a bench. Lay down the first sheet of filo pastry, shortest side towards you, and brush lightly with melted butter. Lay a second sheet of filo pastry over the top and brush with butter. Repeat with the third and fourth sheets.

Spoon the filling in a thick sausage along the short side of the pastry sheets, leaving a border at the end and on the long sides. Fold the long sides in over the filling. Carefully roll up the filo from the short side to form a log-shaped packet.

>

Slide onto a baking tray. Sprinkle with icing sugar and bake for 15 minutes.

Reduce the oven temperature to 180°C and bake for a further 15–20 minutes or until the pastry is brown and crisp.

Cool a little before cutting with a serrated knife. Dust with icing sugar before serving.

# ✍ English Sherry Trifle

## Serves 6–8

*1 small, plain sponge cake*
*2–3 tablespoons strawberry or raspberry jam*
*1½ cups medium dry sherry*
*8 amaretti biscuits (almond macaroons), crushed*
*250 ml cream*
*500 ml vanilla custard*
*2 tablespoons toasted flaked almonds*

Cut the cake in half and spread the jam between the layers.
Cut into small chunks to fit into the bottom of an
attractive glass bowl or dish. Pour the sherry over the top
and set aside for 30 minutes.

Sprinkle with the crushed amaretti biscuits. Whip the
cream until stiff and mix half of it carefully through the
custard. Pour the custard over the sponge and biscuits and,
using a piping bag, pipe the rest of the cream to decorate
the top. Sprinkle the toasted flaked almonds over the top.

Refrigerate for 1 hour before serving.

# ✹ Fresh Plum Tart with Crumble Topping

## Serves 6

*1 cup castor sugar*
*pinch of salt*
*125 g chilled butter*
*1¼ cups plain flour*
*½ teaspoon ground cinnamon*
*¼ teaspoon baking powder*
*2 eggs*
*¼ cup castor sugar*
*½ cup sour cream*
*½ teaspoon vanilla extract*
*12 dark plums, stones removed and each one cut into eight*
*icing sugar, for dusting*

Preheat the oven to 180°C. Lightly grease a 20-cm tart tin.

Combine the sugar, salt, butter and flour in a food processor and pulse until the butter is mixed into the flour and the mixture resembles coarse breadcrumbs. Divide the mixture into two. Add the cinnamon and baking powder to one mixture. Lightly beat one egg and stir into the mixture to form a sticky ball. Press into the base of the tart tin and cook for 10 minutes or until just set.

Meanwhile, whisk the other egg with ¼ cup castor sugar, sour cream and vanilla extract.

Remove the base from the oven and arrange the plums over the top. Pour the egg custard mixture over the plums. Take the remaining flour-and-butter mixture and sprinkle it over the top.

Return to the oven and bake for 20–30 minutes or until lightly browned. Cool a little.

Dust with icing sugar and serve with Pouring Custard (see page 10) or cream.

## ❧ Fruity Christmas Pudding

### Serves 12 (makes 2 × 600 g puddings)

*150 g raisins*
*150 g sultanas*
*80 g currants*
*50 g mixed peel*
*50 g dried apple, chopped*
*25 g prunes, stones removed and roughly chopped*
*25 g dates, stones removed and roughly chopped*
*50 ml rum*
*30 ml dark ale*
*125 g butter*
*100 g brown sugar*
*40 g peeled carrot, finely grated*
*20 g flour*
*40 g almonds, finely chopped*
*1 tablespoon dark treacle*
*½ teaspoon mixed spice*
*¼ teaspoon ground nutmeg*
*1 egg*
*60 g fresh breadcrumbs*
*140 g dried breadcrumbs*

Combine the dried fruit in a large bowl and pour the rum and dark ale over the top. Leave to marinate for 1 day.

Melt the butter and brown sugar. Pour the mixture over

the fruit and stir in the rest of the ingredients. Mix well with a spoon or use your hands. Divide the mixture into half and form into two balls. Place each pudding into a baking bag and tie with string, leaving room for the pudding to swell a little.

Suspend in a pot of simmering water and cook, covered, for 2½ hours. Remove and leave to cool. To reheat, cook in the bag for 40 minutes or until the pudding is heated through.

Serve warm with Pouring Custard (see page 10) – perhaps with a splash of rum added – or ice-cream.

# ❧ Gingerbread and Rhubarb Pudding

## Serves 6–8

*110 g softened butter*
*110 g brown sugar*
*2 eggs, lightly beaten*
*225 g treacle*
*1 teaspoon ground ginger*
*225 g plain flour*
*1 level teaspoon bicarbonate of soda*
*4 tablespoons milk*
*450 g rhubarb, chopped into small pieces*
*icing sugar, for dusting*

Preheat the oven to 180°C. Grease a 1.5-litre ovenproof dish.

Cream the butter and sugar until light and fluffy. Slowly add the eggs. Pour in the treacle and mix well. Sift the ginger and the flour and stir into the batter. Dissolve the bicarbonate of soda in the milk and stir in. Spoon one-third of the mixture into the prepared dish and sprinkle with rhubarb. Spoon the rest of the batter over the top.

Bake for 45 minutes; then reduce the oven temperature to 160°C. Loosely cover the top of the pudding with foil and bake for a further 30 minutes.

Dust with icing sugar before serving with ice-cream or whipped cream.

# ❧ Individual Baked Alaskas

## Serves 4

### Chocolate Brownie Base

125 g butter
90 g cooking chocolate, broken into small pieces
2 eggs
²/₃ cup sugar
90 g chopped pecan nuts
1 cup plain flour
¼ cup milk

### Meringue Mixture

2 egg whites
¼ teaspoon cream of tartar
¼ cup castor sugar
4 large scoops of chocolate ice-cream

Preheat the oven to 180°C. Line a 30-cm × 20-cm shallow baking dish with non-stick baking paper.

Melt the butter and chocolate in a saucepan over low heat, stirring occasionally. Remove from heat and cool a little.

Using an electric mixer, whisk the eggs and sugar together until pale and thick. Combine the nuts and sifted flour and add to the egg mixture, along with the melted chocolate and butter. Stir to combine and then stir in the milk.

Pour into the prepared dish and bake for 25–30 minutes, or until cooked through. Cool in the tin for 15 minutes; then place on a rack.

To make the meringue mixture, place the 2 egg whites in a bowl with the cream of tartar and whisk with an electric beater until soft peaks form. Add in the castor sugar one spoonful at a time until the meringue mixture is shiny.

To assemble
Preheat the oven to 220°C.

Scoop 4 large helpings of chocolate ice-cream onto a small baking tray and place in the freezer until ready to use.

Cut 4 even-sized pieces of brownie base to fit under the ice-cream scoops and place onto non-stick baking paper on a baking tray. (Cut the remaining brownie base into small squares and store for future use.)

Remove the ice-cream from the freezer and place on top of the brownie base. Using a spatula, spread the meringue carefully all over the ice-cream and brownie, making sure there is no ice-cream or base showing.

Bake for 3–4 minutes or until the meringue is lightly browned. Serve immediately.

# ❧ Individual Bread Puddings

### Serves 6

*6 slices of day-old white bread, torn into small pieces*
*300 ml milk*
*1 large apple, peeled, cored and grated*
*1 cup mixed dried fruit, finely chopped (pears, apples,*
*    sultanas, raisins)*
*4 tablespoons mixed peel*
*2 tablespoons brown sugar*
*2 tablespoons dark orange marmalade*
*4 tablespoons self-raising flour*
*2 eggs, beaten*
*1 teaspoon lemon juice*
*1 teaspoon ground cinnamon*
*1 teaspoon mixed spice*
*60 g melted butter*
*icing sugar, for dusting*

Preheat the oven to 150°C. Lightly grease 6 ramekin dishes.
   Combine the bread and milk and leave to soak until soft
(about 20 minutes). Beat well with a fork to form a
smooth puree.
   Add the apple, mixed dried fruit and mixed peel. Stir in
the sugar, marmalade, sifted flour, eggs, lemon juice,
cinnamon spice and mixed spice. Pour half of the melted
butter into the mixture and stir well.

Spoon the pudding into the 6 ramekin dishes and drizzle the rest of the butter over the top.

Bake for 45 minutes–1 hour or until lightly browned and firm to the touch. Cool a little. Dust with icing sugar and serve with Pouring Custard (see page 10).

# Individual Sticky Date Puddings with Hot Butterscotch Sauce

## Serves 6

1¼ cups chopped, dried dates
1¼ cups water
1 teaspoon bicarbonate of soda
60 g softened butter
¾ cup castor sugar
2 eggs, lightly beaten
1 cup self-raising flour

Hot Butterscotch Sauce
125 ml cream
100 g butter
½ cup brown sugar

Preheat the oven to 180°C. Lightly oil a 6-cup jumbo muffin tin.

Place the dates and water in a saucepan and bring to the boil, simmering for about 5 minutes or until the dates are softened. Remove from the heat and stir in the bicarbonate of soda.

Cream the butter and sugar until light and fluffy. Add the eggs a little at a time, beating after each addition to make a smooth batter. Fold in the sifted flour; then stir in the date-and-water mixture until well combined.     >

Spoon into the prepared muffin cups and bake for
20 minutes or until firm and springy to touch.

To make the sauce, combine all the ingredients in a
saucepan and stir over a low heat until the butter is melted.
Simmer for 10 minutes or until thickened.

Turn the puddings out and serve warm on individual
plates with Butterscotch Sauce poured over the top.

# Italian Rice Tart

### Serves 6

*200 g plain flour*
*75 g chilled butter, cut into small pieces*
*1 egg, lightly beaten with 2 tablespoons very cold water*
*1 litre milk*
*180 g castor sugar*
*1 teaspoon vanilla essence*
*100 g short-grain rice*
*grated zest of 1 lemon*
*30 g pine nuts*
*20 g currants*
*50 g fresh or frozen blackberries*
*icing sugar, for dusting*

Preheat the oven to 180°C. Lightly grease a 23-cm flan
dish.

Sift the flour into a food processor, add the chilled butter
and blend until the mixture resembles fine breadcrumbs.
Pour in the egg and water and process until just combined.
Add more chilled water if necessary. Remove and knead
lightly.

Roll out the pastry and use it to line the prepared dish.
Chill in the fridge while you make the rice filling.          >

In a saucepan, bring the milk to the boil with the sugar
and vanilla essence. Add the rice and cook for 20 minutes
at a simmer. Remove and pour into a mixing bowl.
Stir in the lemon zest, pine nuts, currants and blackberries.
Leave to cool. Pour into the prepared dish and bake for
30 minutes or until set and lightly browned on top.
Cool completely before cutting.

Dust the top with icing sugar or serve with a puree
of strawberries or raspberries.

# 🐝 Lemon Delicious Pudding

## Serves 6

*60 g unsalted butter*
*85 g castor sugar*
*85 g self-raising flour*
*grated zest of 2 lemons*
*juice of 1 lemon*
*2 eggs, separated*
*300 ml milk*

Preheat the oven to 180°C. Lightly grease a 1-litre ovenproof dish.

Cream the butter and sugar until light and fluffy. Sift in the flour, and add the lemon zest and juice. Whisk the egg yolks and milk and mix into the pudding batter until well combined. Whip the egg whites until stiff and carefully fold them into the pudding mixture.

Spoon the pudding mixture into the prepared dish and place in a baking dish half-filled with boiling water. Bake for 30–35 minutes or until the sponge on top is golden.

Serve immediately.

## ⌘ Lemon Meringue Pie

Serves 8

Pastry
100 g very cold butter
225 g plain flour
1 teaspoon grated lemon zest
50 g icing sugar
1 egg, lightly beaten
2–3 tablespoons very cold water

Filling
½ cup cornflour
1 cup castor sugar
½ cup lemon juice
1¼ cups water
3 large eggs, separated
60 g butter
½ cup castor sugar, extra

Preheat the oven to 220°C. Lightly grease a 24-cm flan dish.

Using a food processor, pulse the butter and flour until the mixture resembles fine breadcrumbs. Add the lemon zest and icing sugar and pulse for 1 minute.

Combine the egg and water and, with the motor running, slowly pour enough liquid into the food processor for the mixture to come together. Remove and roll into a ball. Chill for 30 minutes.

On a floured board, roll out the pastry to fit the flan dish. Blind bake (see page 4) for 10–15 minutes or until lightly browned. Remove from the oven and reduce the oven temperature to 180°C.

In a saucepan, combine the cornflour and sugar and slowly stir in the lemon juice and water. Stir over a low heat until the mixture comes to the boil. Continue stirring until the mixture thickens. Remove from the heat and whisk in the egg yolks and butter. Cool, covered with greaseproof paper, until ready to use.

Whisk the egg whites until soft peaks form; then slowly add the extra castor sugar until the egg whites are stiff and glossy.

Spoon the filling onto the pastry shell and spread evenly. Spoon the meringue over the top and bake on a preheated baking tray for 10–15 minutes or until the meringue is lightly browned.

Serve warm or cold with pouring cream.

# ✀ Lemony Treacle Tart

Serves 8

Pastry
150 g very cold butter
300 g plain flour
1 teaspoon grated lemon zest
50 g icing sugar
1 egg, lightly beaten
2–3 tablespoons very cold water
100 g fresh breadcrumbs

Filling
3 eggs, lightly beaten
finely grated zest and juice of 1 lemon
350 ml golden syrup
150 ml cream
150 ml milk

Preheat the oven to 180°C. Lightly grease a deep 23-cm loose-bottomed tart tin.

Using a food processor, pulse the butter and flour until the mixture resembles fine breadcrumbs. Add the lemon zest and icing sugar and pulse for 1 minute.

Combine the egg and water and, with the motor running, slowly pour liquid into the food processor until

the mixture comes together. Remove and roll into a ball.
Chill for 30 minutes.

On a floured board, roll out the pastry to fit the tart tin.
Trim any excess pastry. Blind bake (see page 4) for 10–15
minutes or until lightly golden. Remove from the oven and
then reduce the oven temperature to 170°C.

Sprinkle the breadcrumbs over the prepared pastry shell.
Combine all the filling ingredients in a food processor and
blend until smooth. Pour into the tart tin and bake for
35 minutes or until the filling is golden and puffed up.

Cool in the tin before turning out and serving.

# ⌇ Little Chocolate Self-saucing Puddings

## Serves 8

*110 g dark chocolate*
*115 g butter*
*4 eggs*
*130 g castor sugar*
*60 g plain flour*
*20 g ground almonds*

Preheat the oven to 160°C. Lightly grease 8 × 125-ml
ramekin or pudding bowls.

Melt the chocolate and butter in a small saucepan over a
gentle heat. Leave to cool.

Using an electric mixer, beat the eggs and sugar until
pale and thick (3–4 minutes). Combine the sifted flour
and almonds and carefully fold into the egg mixture.

Gently fold through the chocolate mixture. Spoon into
the prepared bowls and bake for 15–20 minutes or until
just cooked but still a little soft in the middle.

Serve warm, turned out onto individual plates, with
Pouring Custard (see page 10) or pureed raspberries.

# ✎ Little Orange Sponge Puddings with Rhubarb Sauce

## Serves 6

*2 tablespoons butter*
*¾ cup castor sugar*
*zest of 2 oranges*
*¼ teaspoon salt*
*3 large eggs, separated*
*½ cup orange juice*
*½ cup milk*
*3 tablespoons plain flour*

Preheat the oven to 180°C. Lightly grease 6 × 125-ml ramekin dishes or tea cups and sprinkle a little castor sugar inside to coat the sides and base.

Cream the butter and ¼ cup of the sugar until light and fluffy. Add the orange zest, salt and egg yolks and beat well. Mix in the orange juice, milk and sifted flour. In another bowl, whisk the egg whites until soft peaks form; then slowly whisk in the remaining castor sugar.

Gently fold the egg whites into the egg-yolk mixture. Spoon into the prepared dishes and place in a bain marie (see page 4). Bake for 35 minutes or until the puddings have puffed up. Place puddings on a rack (they will sink a little as they cool). Turn them out onto individual plates and serve with a spoonful of Rhubarb Sauce (see page 11).

# ❧ Pear, Ginger and Raisin Crumble

## Serves 8

Fruit Mixture
1½ kg ripe pears, peeled, cored and cut into small chunks
½ cup brown sugar
½ cup raisins
2 tablespoons plain flour, sifted
2 tablespoons sherry
1 tablespoon finely chopped crystallised ginger

Topping
1 cup plain flour
1 cup walnuts, finely chopped
⅔ cup soft brown sugar
120 g butter, cut into tiny pieces

Preheat the oven to 190°C. Lightly grease a 2-litre ovenproof dish.

Combine all the Fruit Mixture ingredients and spoon into the prepared dish.

Combine the flour, walnuts, sugar and butter until the mixture starts to clump together.

Spoon the topping over the pears and bake for 30 minutes or until the topping is golden and crisp.

Cool a little before serving with plain yogurt or Pouring Custard (see page 10).

# ❧ Prune and Apple Frangipane Tart

## Serves 8

### Pastry
*2 cups plain flour*
*½ cup sugar*
*180 g chilled butter*
*1 egg, lightly beaten*

### Filling
*200 g flaked almonds*
*1 cup sugar*
*4 eggs*
*225 g softened butter*
*1 tablespoon rum*
*½ teaspoon vanilla extract*
*½ teaspoon almond extract*
*16 dried pitted prunes, soaked in hot tea for 20 minutes*
*1 Granny Smith apple, peeled, cored and cut into 16 slices*

Preheat the oven to 180°C. Line a 30-cm × 25-cm baking tray with non-stick baking paper.

Using a food processor, mix the flour and sugar together. Add the chilled butter and pulse until the mixture resembles coarse breadcrumbs. Add the egg and process for 1–2 minutes or until the pastry forms a ball. Pat pastry into the base of the prepared tray. Blind bake (see page 4) for >

8–10 minutes or until golden and firm. Cool a little while you prepare the filling.

Combine the almonds and sugar in a food processor and process for 2 minutes. Add the eggs, butter, rum, vanilla and almond extracts and process until creamy. Spread evenly over the pastry. Arrange the prunes and apple slices over the top.

Bake for 25–30 minutes or until lightly browned and cooked through.

Cut into squares and serve warm with whipped cream or plain yogurt.

# ❧ Rhubarb and Ricotta Crumble

## Serves 6

Crumble
*150 g butter*
*150 g plain flour*
*150 g soft brown sugar*
*100 g rolled oats*

Rhubarb and Ricotta Filling
*500 g ricotta cheese*
*3 eggs*
*4 tablespoons castor sugar*
*2 tablespoons orange juice*
*400 g cooked rhubarb, pureed*

Preheat the oven to 180°C. Lightly grease a 23-cm springform pan.

Combine the butter, flour, brown sugar and rolled oats in a food processor and pulse until the mixture starts to clump together. Reserve ¾ of a cup of the mixture, and press the rest into the prepared pan. Bake for 15–20 minutes or until lightly browned and firm.

Meanwhile, combine the ricotta, eggs, castor sugar and orange juice. Mix well until smooth.

Spread the pureed rhubarb over the baked crumble base. Pour in the ricotta. Sprinkle the reserved crumble over, and bake for 35–40 minutes. Cool to room temperature.

# ⌘ Simple Tarte Tatin

## Serves 6

*100 g brown sugar*
*½ teaspoon ground cardamom*
*100 g butter*
*6–8 Golden Delicious apples, peeled, cored and quartered*
  *lengthways*
*1 sheet ready-rolled frozen puff pastry, thawed*

Preheat the oven to 220°C.

Sprinkle the sugar and cardamom over the bottom of a
24-cm ovenproof frying pan or skillet and dot with the
butter.

Tightly pack the apple quarters into the pan, with the
rounded sides pressed down into the sugar.

Cook over a high heat until the sugar and butter
caramelises the apples. Remove from the heat and place the
puff pastry on top, trimming the edges a little.

Bake on a preheated oven tray for 10–15 minutes or
until the pastry is cooked. Remove from the oven and cool
a little. Invert the tart onto a plate and serve with Pouring
Custard (see page 10) or cream.

# ❦ Upside-down Caramel Banana Pudding

### Serves 6

*60 g butter*
*60 g brown sugar*
*3 large ripe bananas, thinly sliced*
*4 tablespoons walnut halves*
*250 g softened butter*
*250 g brown sugar*
*200 g self-raising flour*
*2 level teaspoons baking powder*
*50 g chopped walnuts*
*3 tablespoons milk*

Preheat the oven to 180°C. Lightly grease a 2-litre shallow ovenproof dish or cake tin.

Melt the butter and sugar in a saucepan over a low heat. Spread over the base and sides of the dish and lay the banana slices over the top. Squeeze the walnut halves into any gaps.

Blend the rest of the ingredients together in a food processor or using an electric mixer. Spread the mixture over the bananas and bake for 50 minutes or until the pudding is cooked through and golden brown on top. Run a knife around the edges and turn out onto a hot dish.

Serve warm or cold.

# ✒ Warm Upside-down Ricotta Cakes with Melba Sauce

## Serves 6

Base
*1 cup plain sweet biscuit crumbs*
*60 g softened butter*

Filling
*¼ cup cream cheese*
*1 cup ricotta cheese*
*½ teaspoon vanilla extract*
*½ teaspoon almond extract*
*2 large eggs, lightly beaten*
*3 tablespoons castor sugar*

Preheat the oven to 180°C. Lightly grease a 6-cup jumbo muffin tin.

Combine the biscuit crumbs and butter and press into the bases of the muffin cups.

Beat the filling ingredients until smooth. Spoon evenly into the muffin cups. Bake for 15–20 minutes or until set. Cool for 10 minutes before turning out.

Serve upside down, drizzled with Melba Sauce (see page 9).

# ❧ Wicked Marbled Chocolate Pudding

## Serves 6

*50 g dark chocolate*
*50 g white chocolate*
*110 g softened butter*
*110 g brown sugar*
*2 eggs, beaten*
*110 g self-raising flour*

Preheat the oven to 190°C, or fill a steaming pan with water. Lightly grease a 900-ml pudding basin.

Melt the chocolates separately in bowls over hot water.

Cream the butter and sugar until light and fluffy. Add the eggs, a little at a time; then fold in the sifted flour. Spoon half of the mixture into another bowl and stir in the melted dark chocolate. Stir the white chocolate into the other half of the mixture. Spoon the white and dark chocolate mixtures into the prepared basin alternatingly. Using a wooden skewer, swirl through the mixture to create a marbled effect.

Cover with buttered, pleated foil. Steam for 1½ hours on top of the stove, topping up with water as necessary, or bake for 1½ hours.

Turn out and serve with Hot Chocolate Sauce (see page 8).

# INDEX